I Spy a Re[ptile]

by Isabel Thomas

Say the sounds.

/igh/ -y i i-e
/oa/ o ou -oe o-e -ough -eau

Blend the sounds to read the words.

doughnut   snow   lie   plateau
backbone   boulder   wild   gecko
glide   toes

I spy a reptile!
There are lots of different kinds of reptiles.

To find a reptile you need to look for:

backbone

dry skin

scales

Most wild reptiles live alone.
They like to hide!

python

There are lots to find in this book!

Can you spy a reptile? Where is it?

Clue: Look beside the **boulder**. It is hiding.

Reptiles cannot control their body temperature like us. They lie in a shady spot when they need to cool down.

Can you find a reptile? Where is it?

Clue: Look on the bark.

This reptile looks like it can fly!

Can you spy a reptile? Where is it?

Clue: Look behind the strawberries.

This gecko is at home in the heat!
Geckoes have sticky toes!

Can you find a reptile? Where is it?

Clue: Look beside the road. It is waiting to cross.

11

Komodo dragons look terrifying!
If people get too close, they will strike.
Experts think their bite might be **toxic**.

Komodo dragon

Can you spy a reptile? Where is it?

Clue: Look for a tail in the snow.

When it's cold, reptiles cope by going slowly.

garter snake

I curl up like a doughnut and doze!

Can you find a reptile? Where is it?

Clue: Look under a log.

This reptile can drop its tail!
Predators such as snakes find the tail.

They don't find the rest of me!

blue-tailed skink

Can you spy a reptile? Where is it?

Clue: Try the pond! Focus on the lilies.

Turtle shells do not float on their own.

Can you find a reptile? Where is it?

Clue: Look at the stones near the slope.

This is called a toad-head lizard!
It lives on a high **plateau**.

Reptiles hide when they are frightened. Some hide when they are waiting to strike!

green sand lizard

Did you find all the reptiles in the book?

Glossary

backbone: the line of bones along the reptile's back

boulder: a very big rock

glide: fly smoothly in the air without flapping wings

plateau: a bit of land that is flat and high

toxic: harmful, like poison

Talk together

1. How does the flying dragon glide without wings?

2. When do reptiles need to find a shady spot?

3. Match the reptiles to their habitats.